Cats

CATS

Art, Legend, History

Fabio Amodeo
Series editor: Giorgio Coppin

The Bulfinch Library of Collectibles

A Bulfinch Press Book
Little, Brown and Company
Boston · Toronto · London

First North American Edition

English translation by Ardèle Dejey
Series editor: Giorgio Coppin

Library of Congress Cataloging-in-Publication Data

Amodeo, Fabio.
[Gatto. English]
Cats: art, legend, history/Fabio Amodeo.—1st North American ed.
p. cm. —(The Bulfinch library of collectibles)
"A Bulfinch Press book."
ISBN 0-8212-2008-X
1. Cats—Collectibles. 2. Cats—Legends. 3. Cats—History.
I. Title. II. Series.
NK3896.A4813 1992
704.9'432—dc20 92-30653

Bulfinch Press is an imprint and trademark of Little, Brown and Company (Inc.)
Published simultaneously in Canada by Little, Brown & Company (Canada) Limited

PRINTED IN ITALY

CONTENTS

For four thousand years the cat has shared man's home without relinquishing one iota of its independence; a position of privilege that is due to its magical powers of seduction which even the hardest heart cannot resist. This perfect example in china of an irresistible little mouser comes from Germany.

Who domesticated who?

The very first question I would pose about cats would be this: how is it that the apparently least tameable animal in the entire world has come to be such a popular pet and loving companion? But perhaps the question needs rephrasing. To understand what I mean, cast an eye at your own cat, reflect for an instant on its habits, and on the last time you tried to get it to do something that it did not wholeheartedly agree with. You will see how the question immediately changes. In all honesty can we really say we are sure that the cat is a domestic animal in the accepted sense of the word? Are we really convinced that cohabitation was a deliberate choice on its part or is it just that a cat's habitat merely coincides with our house and the immediate surroundings?

Talking to cat owners does nothing to resolve this doubt. Cat lovers are, on this subject, completely unreliable. They take as marks of affection what any impartial observer would identify as manifestations of self-interest, prudent actions designed to assure adequate supplies of food and comfort. They tell of the long conversations they have with their pet but omit to mention the times when the cat's reaction to

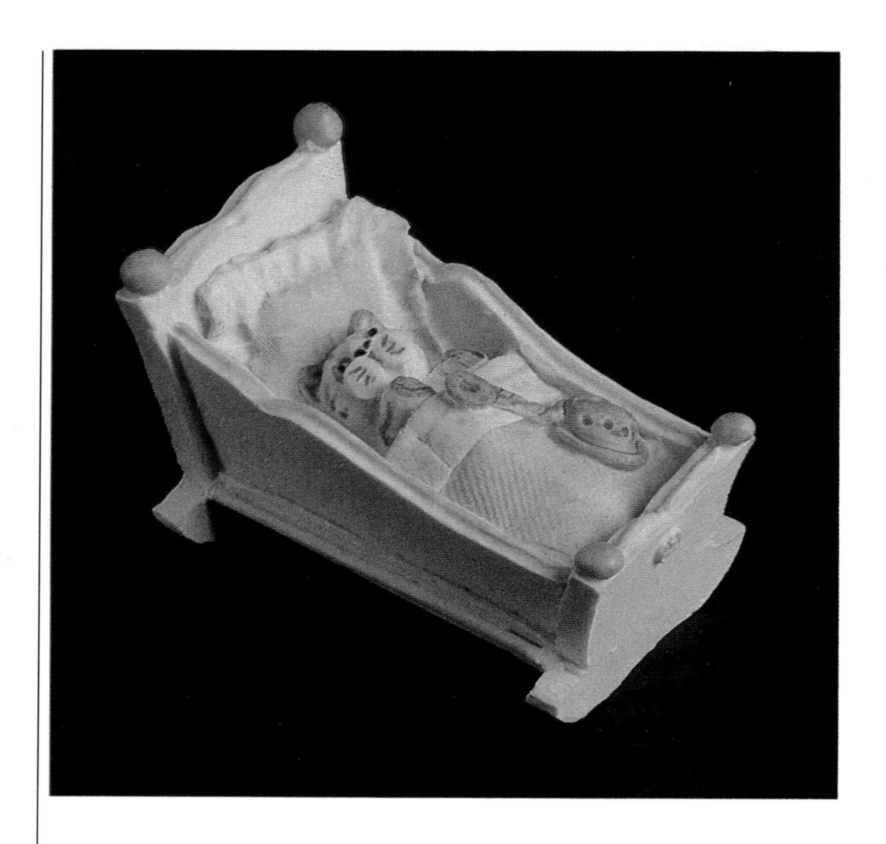

their attempts to stroke and cuddle it was to turn round and go back to sleep. Let us be truthful. Let us try to be objective and ask ourselves if we can call "domestic" an animal whose idea of a typical day is as follows: to spend two-thirds of the available time asleep; to find a comfortable spot in which to lie in the sun for a couple of hours; to pass another hour or two gazing out of the window or from the garden wall; to wash carefully from nose to tail at least twice, with suitable profligacy of time; to ask for food a number of times throughout the day, varying from three to twenty, with proportional use of mewing and rubbing; to eat; and, finally, to perform social activities that entail games with whatever will roll about, preferably precious objects, for a good twenty minutes. Well, does this seem to be the diary of an animal that can seriously be defined as domesticated?

Cat lovers will retort that only this pet is capable of gestures of infinite tenderness, such as curling itself into a ball on the lap of whoever is watching television, often purring as a sign of great contentment. It is useless trying to explain to them that their dear pussy cat shows equal affection for any source of warmth, from the fireplace to the stove, to the cashmere cardigan left forgotten on a chair.

Therefore, the real question is this: how has the cat, for so long, made generations of humans wrongly interpret simple acts of self-interested cohabitation as domesticity?

What magic power has the feline to make a normally independent being like Homo sapiens completely dependent on it, without itself forfeiting one ounce of its own independence? Perhaps the secrets of the cat lie wholly in the realm of magic. Watch it while it moves, while it runs, while it makes the most simple movements and, the most amazing, when from complete immobility it suddenly

Cats are very popular pets but kittens perhaps have an even greater appeal as seen in these delightful Italian porcelains. Opposite, a small hand-painted English piece in resin from the Peter Fagan Collection.

springs into an armchair. Watch those eyes that look like small windows on the unknowable.

Think of the notoriety that surrounds it – a reputation earned by every cat you know: its nine lives; its leaping and balancing skills and its amazing ability always to land on its paws; and its sense of direction that enables it to always find its way home from wherever it may have managed to end up, or from wherever someone has tried to abandon it (fortunately nowadays the world is pretty well divided between people who would never let a cat inside their own homes, and those who think it criminal to leave their cat outside the front door).

In short, without becoming obsessive about a pervasive whiff of brimstone, as indeed happened in Europe for several centuries, there has always been a degree of uneasiness in defining a cat's nature. This is probably due to certain unsettling forms of behaviour common to all these creatures: cats will either reject your attentions with a nervous eye or totally embrace your companionship and never leave your side. While these extremes seem excessive, they are part of our companion's ways, characteristics that

One of the reasons for the cat's popularity in the home is its ability to entertain children, as this Italian postcard from the 1920s shows. Opposite, a wooden kitty by a Mexican sculptor. The large rocking-cat on the preceding pages is early twentieth century.

we would even like to share, strengths that elude man's more fickle ways.

The cat's constant sense of dignity; its reserve; its ability to be totally independent or to "walk by itself," in the words of Kipling's marvellous story, and never to be worried by its solitude; its capacity to make up its own mind; its composure; its imperviousness to events yet with an extraordinary aptitude for instant reaction – all this is part of the cat, of every cat, even if our feline friends do differ immensely from one another. All these attributes we, ourselves, would like to have but never shall. And there, possibly, lies the answer to our initial question. Man and cat started to live together through common interest. The cat, perhaps, found comfortable surroundings without losing one iota of freedom and independence. Man, living with the cat, could perhaps study at close quarters the creature he himself would like to be, endowed with gifts he coveted but which may be beyond his reach.

When and how this domestication first occurred is

At least in sculpted form the cat is quiet and controllable and is, therefore, a perfect ornament, like the nineteenth-century china tableware above, or the cat in hardstone from Kenya opposite.

uncertain. The cat emerged on to the scene in an impressive way in ancient Egypt. It is generally believed that, at some point, some kittens of *Felis silvestris libyca*, the wild cat that roamed over North Africa, were taken into houses along the banks of the Nile and that these became the forebears of *Felis domesticus* or *Felis cattus*. The remarkable fact remains, however, that outside Egypt in all the great iconographic cycles of prehistory, the cat is conspicuous by its absence: indeed, it seems not worthy of mention, either as a domestic animal or as a wild one, or even as a hunter of vermin.

In the rare findings in prehistoric sites of cats' bones they are mixed up with those of other animals that would form the normal diet of the hunter. This makes it seem that the wild cat of those times, every so often, ended up in the cooking pot, or that its fur helped to stave off the rigours of the cold.

Furthermore, the general belief that the domestication of the cat only dates back to the Middle Kingdom of Egyptian civilization, which in human history is a short time, has been slightly shaken by recent findings. Cats' remains were uncovered in an archaeological dig in Cyprus among items that were dated to about seven thousand years ago. Since we know with reasonable certainty that there were no cats native to Cyprus because no fossils have been found in an otherwise rich inventory, the only conclusion to be drawn is that the cat must have arrived in the wake of Neolithic

More irresistibly charming kittens. The preserve jar above is English, as is the bath tub opposite in hand-painted resin, from the Peter Fagan Collection. The porcelain coffee cup on the preceding pages is nineteenth-century French.

men who landed on the island. It could, of course, be an isolated case.

The remains appear to be those of the African wild cat, *Felis silvestris libyca*; there were none of the typical signs, such as an overall decrease in size and a weakening of some bone structures, that occur within a few generations of domestication. So perhaps these remains are not evidence of pet cats; today there are people who actually live with cheetahs and pythons, and no one could call such animals domestic. So, for the sake of historical argument, let us continue to believe the hypothesis of an African wild cat entering a house on the Nile. But the real question is, why did it stay there?

There are very good reasons for the domestication of all animals. They have been admitted into man's home because they serve certain purposes: food; work; particular skills, such as hunting; and companionship. In some parts of Vietnam there was a market for cats and dogs as food for

The cat's inclination for long naps is a boon for artists and craftsmen, who get the benefit of a still and serene model. So it was for the creator of the example above, in Italian porcelain, from the 1920s. The Russian picture postcard opposite dates from 1904.

special occasions. This has now been made illegal and, although there may still be a black market operating, the penalties for those who are caught are very severe. In the rest of the world man has preferred to raise herbivores such as chickens and cows to eat rather than omnivorous animals such as cats.

So far as helping in the hunt and hard labour go, half an hour with a cat is enough to know that no forefather of his could ever have been subjected to such degrading activities! Easier to imagine a princess put to work than to think of a cat pulling a plough or lying in wait for a partridge for the benefit of a third party. It is also a question of dignity and pride: much better then to return to being *Felis silvestris*, and to pursue one's own interests in the oases of Libya.

Now we are left with two plausible hypotheses. The first is that of specialized work: the cat indeed has a specialization – hunting mice. Today this precious quality can contribute to matters of cleanliness and protection from infection, but for the early agricultural populations it was a question of

survival. Mice constituted a mortal threat, both to the crops, and – more importantly – to the barns where the harvest was stored.

The vocation of some cats, for exterminating mice and rats, must have been immediately clear and a valuable discovery. It was this predisposition that guaranteed the cat's survival in those centuries when, for reasons of superstition or because food was scarce for man let alone animals, attitudes towards them were not for the most part loving.

So this leaves the last hypothesis, that of the cat as a companion. Perhaps the ancient Egyptians had a specific role for the cat in their families. They certainly must have shared the same problems as those of all families today: young children need constant attention. Television not having been invented, we can be sure that there was therefore a great demand for child care around the Nile, and a little kitten is the most entertaining nanny available. Then of course it grows and the family is stuck with it, but that is another story.

Another example of the sure-fire combination of kittens and babies is seen in this china feeding bottle, made in the early 1980s, by the Florentine craftsman, Armani.

As soon as the cat became domesticated in Egypt four thousand years ago, its career took off to a dazzling start. Here is a sculpture in hardstone of the divinity Bastet, goddess of love and fertility, as well as a great seductress.

And before long a deity

However the introduction of the cat to Egyptian domestic life happened, the rise of the cat in Egypt was quite simply meteoric. Within a few centuries it became a divinity, unquestionably as a result of that familiarity with the supernatural that seems to be its abiding characteristic. This celestial career began during the Twelfth Dynasty, around 2000 B.C.; it reached its height five hundred years later, and lasted until the Roman Conquest. What happened among the gods was not just a successful coup for cats. Early accounts tell of many other animals, such as crocodiles, that were worshipped in Egypt at that time. Because there were not many of them, they came to be protected by a special social taboo. But few succeeded as the cat did in acquiring the status of a goddess: not just any goddess, but the goddess of love, fertility and childbirth. Its name was Bastet and it was a great enchantress. In short, to the Egyptians, nothing on earth could symbolize the ability to seduce better than the cat. As an archetype it was well conceived; indeed it survives to this day. How many lovers call each other "Pussycat" or "Kitten"? The goddess Bastet must have been

in retirement for quite some time now, but if she were to return, she would be happy with how things have fared.

Bastet was worshipped at a sanctuary at Bubastis, a city in the Nile delta, now vanished. The earliest effigies show her as a woman with the head of a cat; later ones represent her simply as a cat. This is why such a large number of cats have survived for us to see in the form of sculpture, paintings and drawings on papyrus.

There are many stories about Egyptian veneration for the four-footed colleagues of Bastet. To injure or to kill a cat was a capital offense (assuming that the culprit managed to avoid being lynched). Herodotus tells us that in Egypt when the household cat died everyone put on mourning and shaved off their eyebrows as a sign of grief. Then, adds the historian, the deceased cat was carried to the city of Bubastis, embalmed and placed in a sacred sepulcher. What is certain is that for a long time it was strictly forbidden to take a cat out of Egypt. According to the universal laws of smuggling, this automatically meant that it was one of the favourite activities of passing Phoenician sailors. The regulations which were enforced and the determination with which the Egyptians sent their secret agents abroad to try to recover the stolen cats must have greatly added to the animal's prestige around the Mediterranean basin, and the ensuing diffusion of *Felis domesticus*.

The elegant cat below recalls other divinities. The cat's head opposite is much truer to life. It adorns a tape-measure case of the early twentieth century.

Not all sculptures inspired by cats show off the animal's grace. This Italian silver mouser looks somewhat surly.

Sometimes one has the impression that the Egyptians exaggerated. Around 500 B.C. the Persian, Cambyses, surrounded the city of Pelusium (today Tisseh near Port Said), but the city was well defended and its troops and citizens had no intention of surrendering. So Cambyses organized a round-up of cats. A stampede of terrified felines was then made to precede the Persian assault, while the first line of invaders was formed by soldiers with cats tied to their shields. Needless to say, the garrison of Pelusium surrendered so as not to harm a sacred animal: a decision that today's more ardent cat lovers would certainly endorse.

Some such tales of worship have not stood up to modern investigation, however, confirming the fact that the ancients sometimes liked to tell tall stories.

Let us look then at the evidence. Early superficial archaeological investigations uncovered an enormous number of mummified cats, which seems to back up

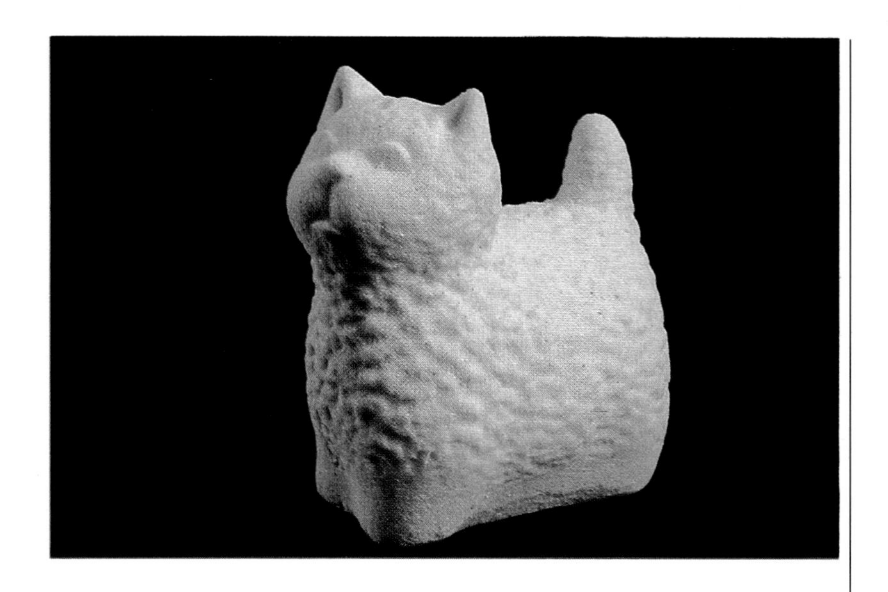

The unmistakable features of a cat make it suited to a very essential style. The Belgian artist who modelled this cat captured these traits in powdered alabaster.

Herodotus's account. Towards the end of the nineteenth century whole shiploads of mummified cats were sent from Egypt, where they did not know what to do with them, to Europe and America, where they were unsure what to do with such quantities. We can imagine the curators of Egyptian museums tearing their hair: "What shall we do? Another box of mummified cats! Where can we put them?"

At some point a good number were sold off cheaply and used as fertilizer. And so, one way and another, not many feline mummies were left. But at the Natural History Museum in London there is a fairly large collection, preserved because, in 1907 along with his other findings, it was donated by the famous Egyptologist, Flinders Petrie (perhaps not even he knew where to put the bandaged bundles). Such an illustrious gift could not be lightly forgotten or left in some basement. There are 190 mummies; of these 187 are recognizable as *Felis silvestris libyca*, which strengthens the theory that this is the ancestor of the domestic cat.

Besides the 190 mummies denuded of their bandages, 55 others of the donation are complete, protected by their cloth wrappings. But a recent investigation using X-rays has shown up some disturbing facts. To start with, the average age of the mummified cats is very young: many between two and four months, most between nine and seventeen months. Only two cats, at the time of their death, were over two years old. This does not seem a great age for such a sacred and protected animal. However, looking more carefully at the X-rays the scholars uncovered another baffling fact: the kittens did not pass into the arms of their

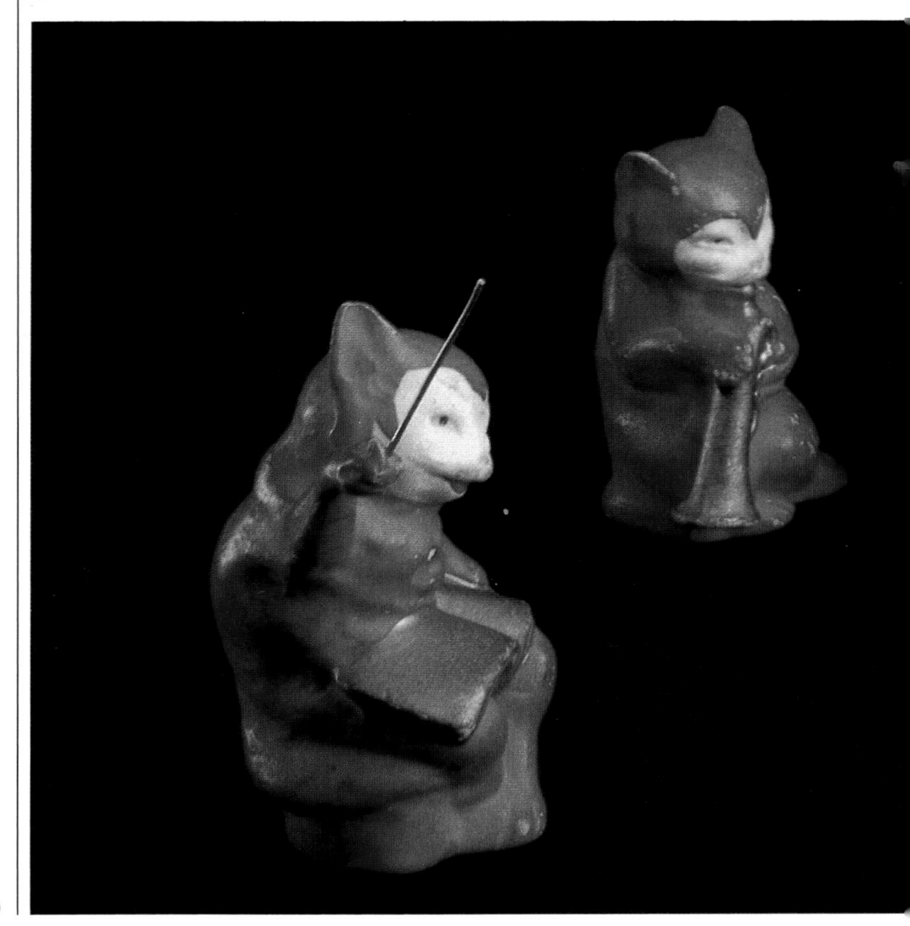

goddess by natural means; most of them had broken necks. They were the victims of a massacre. How could this happen among the amazing cat-loving Egyptians, with the goddess Bastet and all the rest? The most plausible explanation is that the mummies were used by some religious group as cult objects to be placed on an altar in the home during spiritual domestic practices. It is therefore

Feline musicians have yet to be seen, but the artist's imagination knows no limits. This little French orchestra in red biscuit is from the eighteenth century.

likely that older cats, dead from natural causes, and perhaps wasted by a long illness, did not make good mummies. It was clearly much better to breed cats for this end and mummify them when they looked their best.

But, studying the mummies in other museums around the world, one makes another discovery. Often the bandages hide the bones of other animals, or a mixture of bones with pieces of cat. The scholar Wolfgang Pahl recently examined a mummy in the Niagara Falls Museum in Ontario. Together with a cat's remains still under the bindings are bits of human bone. In all probability, the cat worshippers' demands far exceeded the supply. And those vagabonds of priests, so as not to lose their market share, made do with whatever they could.

The Egyptian passion for animals passed as a fashion fad to the Hellenistic world as shown in contemporary mosaics and frescoes. The Romans were too pragmatic and too busy conquering the world to concern themselves with the idea of keeping cats as pets. They limited themselves to going back to using them as exterminators of mice which were, in the meantime, spreading from the Middle East throughout Europe. The time of the Barbaric invasions was not a happy one for our animal, both because the newcomers were even less inclined than the Romans to ask themselves contemplative questions and because they were nomads, the worst possible company for an animal as fundamentally non-migratory as the cat. And yet, by virtue of the law of nine lives, the cat managed fairly well, and at the end of the Dark Ages was still there searching for a warm place in which to have a nap.

In the tenth century during the reign of Hywel Dda, Prince of South Wales and aptly called "the Good," the cat made a comeback and was highly valued. The prince set a

The link between cats and babies knows no frontiers and is found even in the Far East. The Thai carver of this wooden piece was also inspired by the theme, and shows the cat crouching in the lap of a baby.

price on cats: a kitten from birth until its eyes opened was, according to the law, worth "a legal penny"; then up to the time that it killed its first mouse it was worth twopence. After that its value rose to "four legal pence – and at that price it remains." With this evaluation the cat was worth as much as a dog, but far above a piglet, a lamb or a goose, which fetched only one penny. For all that, it was nothing compared to His Majesty's greyhounds quoted at 120 pence. Anyone who killed a cat had to hold the dead animal up by its tail with its head resting on "a clean floor," and pour wheat over the little corpse until it was completely covered up to the tip of its tail. Meanwhile, the European wild cat, with which no doubt the domestic cat of Egyptian origin had regularly mated, was listed in the manuals of behaviour of mediaeval courts. Alas, it was among the quarries of the hunting season, but could be hunted only with seigneurial consent.

During the same period the cat pursued its virtuous career in the East. Mohammed commended its cohabitation with humans and its acceptance in the mosque. Legend has it that the Prophet had a cat of his own. One day when he had to go out he found his cat curled up asleep on his coat. Rather than disturb his beloved mog, Mohammed cut off the sleeve of the garment. On returning home the warm welcome he got from his grateful cat so touched him that he gave cats the right to always fall on their feet, that is, paws down. Cats fared almost as well with Buddha as with the tender-hearted

The cat's exquisite elegance was the ideal inspiration for artists of the Art Deco period, as the French figure below from the 1920s shows. The cat in hardstone opposite is from the East.

Admirers of elegance, the Japanese have always had a great fondness for the domestic cat, as seen in this card from 1904. Maneki-neko, right, is the only cat to have had a temple dedicated to it.

Mohammed. There are two legends, both concerning Buddha's admittance to Nirvana.

Every animal was summoned to attend this event and the first story relates how they all arrived except the cat, the sole absentee, for the simple reason that it had felt like having a nap on the way. This behaviour was not at all well received, and as a result the cat was excluded from the constellations. It is a superb example of feline independence, to be unavailable to pay homage even to Buddha, and no cat has ever lost a moment's sleep because he is not represented in the Chinese calendar. The second legend has a different story with a similar ending. All the animals were gathered round the corpse of the great sage, and all were weeping except the cat and the serpent, a creature not noted for displaying its emotions. The others were inclined to avert their eyes from this indifferent behaviour when a little mouse moved close to the oil lamp illuminating the scene, and began to lick the oil. The cat saw it and – pow! – his

mission was completed. But Buddha had commanded that no animal should ever be killed and, now, here of all places and at such a moment, this wretched cat had to stick its paw in! But cats were soon reinstated. Perhaps the saving of food stores brought recognition of the justice of the cause.

The Japanese have always had an aesthetic fascination for the domestic cat, and it is the artists of Japan who give the truest portrayals of our friend. For a long time, besides being the protagonists of sentimental legends (like that of the loving couple who fled in order to be able to love one another in peace and turned into a pair of cats in order to realize their dream), Japanese cats truly lived like princes. When the emperor Ichijō found a litter of five kittens in a

corner of the palace of Kyoto on the tenth day of the fifth moon of the year 999, which was a time of great spirituality, he guaranteed cats another period of semi-sacredness. This reached the point where, when the cultivation of silkworms was threatened by mice, those responsible were not able to make use of cats (protected by imperial decree), and so decided to substitute strategically placed statuettes of them. Naturally this was to no avail and in the end real cats were put to use, but it took more than two hundred years for Japan to take the decision. Meanwhile, there is in Tokyo the only temple, still in use, dedicated to cats: it is called Go-To-Ku-Ji, and its inhabitant, the gracious Maneki-neko, is always represented with its paw raised in greeting. This cat is surrounded with an aura of magic, but it is white magic. A cat with a front paw raised is the subject of another Japanese legend: a nobleman was riding through a forest when a cat appeared with its paw held up as though to stop him. It led the intrigued rider through the trees to a temple where he found the monks on the point of starvation. The nobleman, of course, immediately called to his retinue to bring food, and not only saved the monks, but saw to it that they never went hungry again. When their cat died they made a little statue of it and it has become a good-luck symbol. More malignant is the ogress-witch in the form of a cat, who creeps into disobedient children's houses to steal and eat them. Such a thing should not be invented to discipline children!

If Neko-Baké is a witch to keep Japanese children good, in Europe for over three centuries the relationship between witches and cats was taken very seriously by adults, so much so that many women and cats were burnt at the stake in what was one of the darkest periods of late mediaeval and modern history. But why, between the end of the

Turning from Japan to the West, Giovanni Thoux, a contemporary sculptor from northwest Italy, created this cat from a root. The carving is minimal and yet it has lost none of its proverbial dignity.

thirteenth century and the end of the seventeenth, did Satan become the obsession of Europe, both Catholic and Protestant? Why were torture and cruelty inflicted on thousands of women, men and innocent cats? There is no unequivocal answer. The one most commonly accepted now is that in a Europe impoverished by the wars and disasters of the thirteenth century, depopulated by the Black Death and rendered spiritually uncertain by the Papal Schism, it became indispensable, for reasons of social order, to identify culprits who eventually came to be sought among the transmitters of popular wisdom, rustic so-called wise women and men, fortune-tellers, herbalists and vagabonds. Later, at the dawn of modern times, the phenomenon was fuelled to eliminate those on the fringe of society, the dissenters, the eccentrics, the disquieting misfits.

Another theory holds that witch-hunting was the ferocious repression of the pantheistic matriarchal cult, widespread since Antiquity throughout Europe and the Mediterranean basin, and extraordinarily deep-rooted in the poorer classes. Indeed the early witch trials saw women confess to meetings and nocturnal flights with groups guided by a lady. In Northern Europe the nocturnal rides through the skies were led by Frejya, by Holda or by Berta who later became Berchta. Frejya and Holda travelled the night sky carried by a group of cats, or in chariots drawn by remarkably robust felines. For a long time, in Scandinavian countries, four bowls of milk were left outside the door at night for the four cats of Frejya. In fact, during the Inquisition all these female divinities were of little interest. First, the inquisitors were unable to admit that a common, popular pagan substratum had survived fifteen centuries of Christianity. Second, their obsession was not pagan rites, but the devil. Apostasy could be pardoned, entailing, at the

Another unlikely feline musician is this nineteenth-century French bronze. The wonderful porcelain cat on the preceding pages was made in Germany.

most, a long series of expiations and penances. To make good bonfires, however, of which judges and inquisitors seemed excessively fond, the direct intervention of the devil was needed. Therefore, confessions were obtained by means of the most atrocious tortures, to the point where over the years and in a sort of unstoppable spiral, the actual beliefs of the victims were influenced and changed into the kind of confessions demanded by the inquisitors. The trouble is that if Berchta or Frejya were superseded by Satan, the cats stayed in the middle, in this case personifications of the devil (especially black cats) or familiars of witches, or what a witch turns into.

Again in the East, the cat reappears in two everyday objects: a papier-mâché box from Nepal, above, and almost unrecognizably as an unusual thimble from China, opposite.

This feline endurance has some interesting aspects. Three thousand years after the Egyptian Bastet, behold! A Mistress Goddess, protectress of fertility, tolerant of female sexuality, reappeared in our civilization. And, at her side, there is always a cat. Is there a line, direct or indirect, between Bastet, the bacchantes of the Classical world and the unfortunate women burnt at the stake in the sixteenth and seventeenth centuries? According to contemporary chroniclers, Bastet's followers, during the yearly pilgrimage, behaved in an unusually immoral way, not very different from those who took part in Dionysian rites. And it certainly cannot be said that the women accused of witchcraft behaved any better during their nocturnal flights.

It is extremely difficult to discover anything about this feline connection because scholarship, always embarrassed by witch-hunting, has pushed it into a corner of its research.

But it is perhaps not an accident that the greatest student of witchcraft, Margaret Murray who, in 1921 wrote *The Witch Cult of Mediaeval Europe* and, ten years later, *The God of the Witches*, besides being a great defender of the cult of the *dea cancellata*, should have been an Egyptologist at University College in London. Nor does it seem an accident that she was badly treated by her contemporaries (mostly male, it seems), who accused her of having created an insufficiently documented hypothesis.

What is certain is that, for cats, the Middle Ages and the Inquisition were the darkest times, to the great relief of rats of course, to such an extent that one marvels that the Black Death and other plagues did not strike more often. The first mass persecution of which we have irrefutable evidence took place in Metz in 962, when hundreds of cats were burned in the course of the pious religious ceremonies of Lent. Pope Gregory IX, sworn enemy of Frederick II of

Swabia, and vigorous defender of the superiority of the Church over the Empire, officially proclaimed the direct link between black cats and the devil. It was a dangerous era, not only for cats; it was enough to own a cat or to have one in the house, to risk serious and woeful consequences. Religious paranoia did not spare even the everlasting rapport between cats and children. In 1699 in the Swedish town of Mora, three hundred children were subjected to a trial for witchcraft. They were accused of using their cats to steal food for the devil. Fifteen boys were condemned to death and thirty-six others were exposed in the public pillory every Sunday for a year. That is what is known as a good education? For a couple of centuries cats appeared in religious paintings: usually in *The Last Supper* and, as a rule, near Judas, just to give an idea of the pervading atmosphere.

This persecution was not confined to Catholics who, under the rule of the Roman Church, counted mogs as devils. Often in Protestant countries led by Luther and Calvin cats were persecuted as personifications of the corrupt Roman Curia. One example suffices: in 1558 the coronation of Elizabeth I of England was celebrated with much festivity. The people showed their joy by making an effigy of the Pope in straw and metal; its interior was crammed with live cats and it was burned, cats and all, at the stake.

In Burgundy too, and in the Vosges and Alsace, religious feasts were often celebrated with the ritual burning alive of cats. In many parts of France it was the custom to sacrifice cats in the fires lit on the eve of St John's feast day. Kings, too, were not above taking part in the sport; Louis XIV, in particular, distinguished himself in this. Little bits of the embers would be carried home as lucky charms. There are even mentions of this dreadful ritual in the National Archive of France: "Payment to Lucas Pommérieux, guardian of the wharves, 100 sous for furnishing for a period of years, ending with the feast of St John 1573, all the cats collected for the usual bonfire, and also for furnishing the large jute bags to carry the aforesaid cats," is written in a receipt signed by this same Lucas Pommérieux. In the town of Ypres the hurling of cats from the towers was in force during Lent. Fortunately it was soon made illegal by a communal law passed in 1618, but still went on from time to time. At Lièges fireworks were dropped with the cats into the flames. The throwing from towers, forbidden at Ypres, survived longer at Korte-Meers: the Flemish, through the "Kattestoët" – meaning "cat throwing" – meant to show their renunciation of Frejya's cult. It is odd that the same ritual intended to honour the cat's fecundity, a quality prized by Flemish girls, is a clear survival from a fertility cult. The "Kattestoët," after alternating interruptions and revivals, was re-established in 1847, with a High Mass amid gala scenes and costumes, which quickly became a great popular procession. The celebration still survives, but happily sanity has prevailed and the cats thrown from the tower are made of cloth. However, ritual sacrifice and the liberating fire were still not the worst possible fate awaiting the cat. In various parts of Europe up to the end of the nineteenth century, there existed the cat

There is a clearly deep fascination in the East with the cat's image. It gives an unusual touch to this padlock-key ring shaped like a nimble cat from India.

organ: a keyboard which, instead of working the pipes of an organ or the hammers of a pianoforte, activated mechanisms that pulled the tails of caged cats, with a view to obtaining unusual sound effects. Afterwards it was the custom for archers to use the cats as moving targets. In Denmark, during tournaments, the "knights" (just horsemen, really, not subscribing to any code of chivalry) stuck their lances into barrels filled with cats.

It is difficult for us to justify such a period of mass sadism. We may conjecture that the general, universal, uncoercible independence of cats was a provocation, especially at a time when humans were themselves frequently deprived of their personal liberty. And other mysteries, such as what are cats thinking about when gazing into space? or where do they go when they disappear into the night?, were not going to aid their fate. To the cat's detriment, also, are its eyes, which are undoubtedly the most mysterious and enigmatic objects in all creation. The great reflective capacity of the retina, from which we catch glimpses of an unfathomable glare, were often interpreted in the past as a reflection of the flames of hell, or as a beam capable of lighting up the dark, a property shared with the devil. This to the point where even today it is a general belief that a cat can see in complete darkness. This is untrue: cats are able to see better than we can with little light, but when there is none at all their eyes are like those of all other creatures, and they must depend on their other senses, in particular hearing and smell.

Finally, another reason for the persecution was the eternal association of felines and female sexuality. In dark times of sex phobia and the absolute subjection of women, no more was required than to be female to give rise to some truly nasty moments. Of course, if women and cats were tormented, another part of the community was able to benefit: that of mice and rats, with all the diseases associated with their spread.

Who has never found their own cat rubbing against the most unlikely objects? This theme was used for this 1930s china vase, with a mouser crouching beside it on a book.

A cat is a cat is a cat is a cat, as Gertrude Stein might have said. Putting this maxim to the proof, an Italian craftsman conceived this unusual metal cat.

Lucky or unlucky?

Official approval of the persecution of cats ceased in the seventeenth century, although it took a long time to erase distrust of the animal from the public's mind. The cat's rehabilitation was slow and was linked to the progress of standards of hygiene and disease prevention. The example of a few enlightened souls such as Cardinal Richelieu, who left a large share of his private fortune to his beloved felines, helped to speed up the cat's reintegration into society.

Above all, we wonder how cats managed to survive the times of persecution. The very fact that they did only seemed to reinforce the myth of their nine lives which was, of course, interpreted as a gift from Satan. So, although the cruelties ceased at a certain period, the superstitions remained. The most cruel belief is from northern Europe, where it was believed that good fortune would come to a house if a live cat was bricked up inside the walls. The corpses of cats, withered by dehydration, have often been found during the demolition of old houses. Sometimes the bodies are in couples, a cat and a mouse, believed to protect against infestation by rodents.

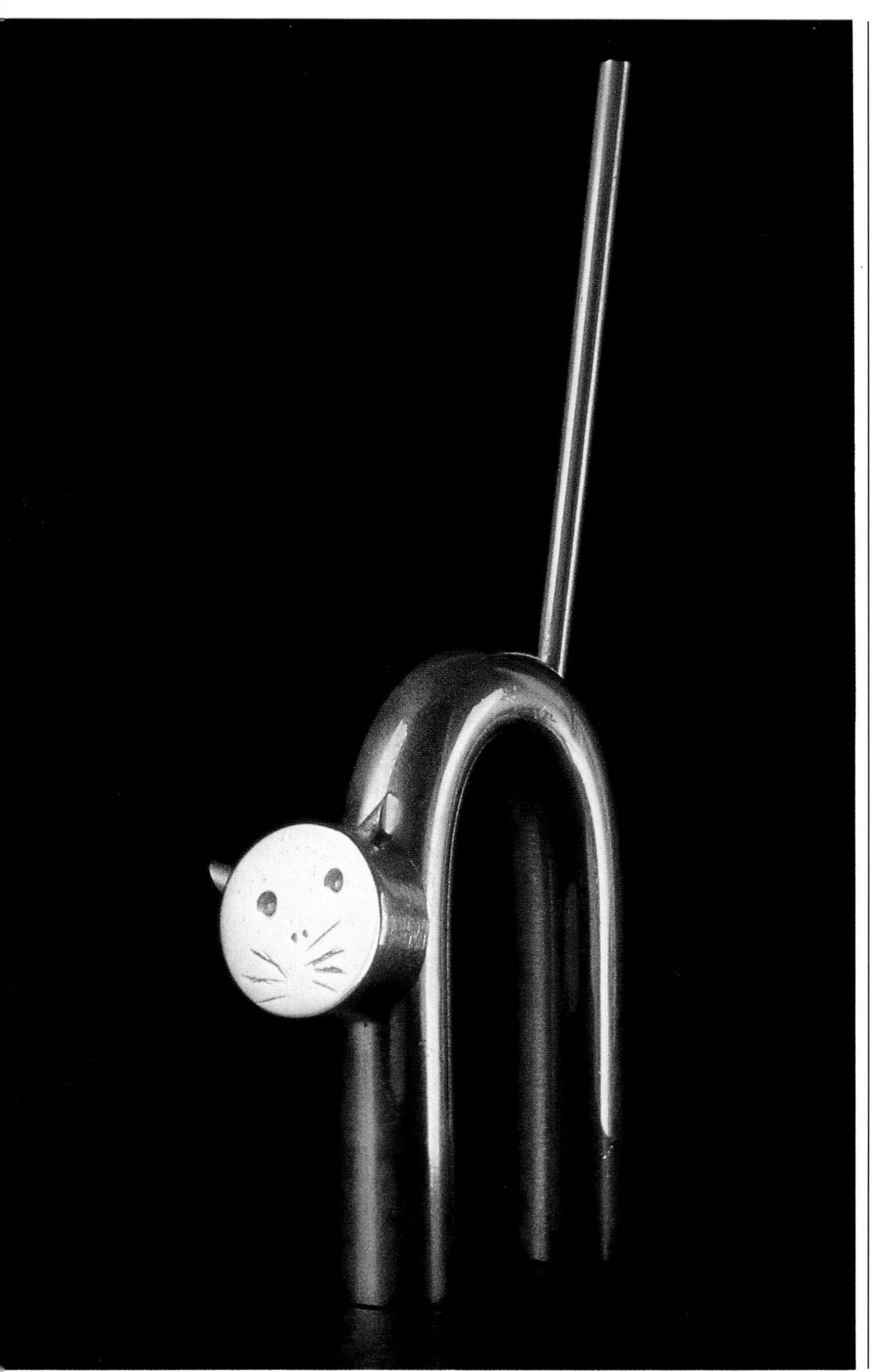

Less macabre superstitions concern the all black or all white cat. In some parts of the United States it is thought to be unlucky if a white kitten enters the house; in Britain, a black cat crossing one's path is believed to bring good luck, but in other countries it heralds misfortune. In Japan it is the tortoiseshell cat that brings good luck.

One beautiful and charming superstition comes from Brittany: every black cat hides a snow-white hair in his fur, just one. If you succeed in finding it and pulling it out without getting scratched you are holding the most effective good-luck charm in the world. The difficult part of this belief is that in order to succeed in finding this hair you must achieve a degree of familiarity that cats rarely concede to humans; you truly need to have the complete confidence of the cat for it to let its fur be searched all over with impunity. There is a moral here: it is always a good thing to make a friend of a cat, even if it is a black one which until not many years ago was an object of suspicion.

There are two more strands of popular belief that are customary almost everywhere. The first concerns the cat's ability to warn of changes in the weather and to signal them by certain behavioural patterns, for example washing its nose early in the morning, chasing its own tail, sneezing, etc. The second, in some ways linked to the first, involves sailors, for whom the cat has always played an important

These cats in terracotta sard seem puzzled. The statuettes are identical, but that on the left is unglazed. The angry puss opposite in silvered porcelain dates from the second half of the nineteenth century.

part, if only in the war against mice. Whatever the reason, sailors have a special predilection anyway for both cats and superstitions, so that every navy traditionally puts its trust in the cat's ability to predict the arrival of a storm. The Scots believe that a storm will be caused if a cat is thrown into the sea. Another seafaring tradition is that a cat flung into the sea will end a dead calm. Usually, however, the relationship between sailors and cats is one of mutual trust and assistance.

So many cats came off galleys and fishing boats into the maritime republic of Venice that, when nearby Vicenza was plagued by hordes of mice, the people ran to Venice for help. The Venetians were happy to supply enough cats to exterminate the mice, but it seems that once they had completed their task the people of Vicenza, instead of returning them, sampled a great many in a variety of recipes. Even today among Venetians, the name *magnagati* (cat-eaters) is used to describe the inhabitants of Vicenza.

A happy seafaring story is that of a young, penniless Londoner, Dick Whittington. Dick was a young boy of ten years and all he possessed in the world was a cat. He found

Who said cats do not like water? The Viennese creator of this bronze from the late nineteenth century has placed two mousers at the oars of this boat, setting off in search of improbable, exotic adventures.

work as an apprentice and did so well that his employer took him along on a trading voyage to the African coast. Naturally, Dick was accompanied by his inseparable grimalkin. In Africa his master sold his cargo at a good price and bought other merchandise. One day he went to the mice-infested palace of the King of Barbary. He thought of Dick's cat, so sent for the boy and the mouser. The cat naturally threw itself at once into its favourite pursuit and the king was so delighted at the result that he offered Dick a huge amount for the animal. Dick was very fond of his cat but, remembering that "business is business," he accepted the offer and returned to London, where he invested his money carefully, founded several businesses under his own name and eventually became, for three consecutive terms, Lord Mayor of London. He is remembered in a statue and a portrait with his cat beside him. Most of this story is untrue, as Dick was really the youngest son of Sir William Whittington of Pauntley in Gloucestershire; he became the richest merchant of his time, trading in coal brought to London in *cats* (sailing boats), a word confused with the

French *achat*, meaning "purchase" or trading at a profit.

We left the history of our feline struggling with a difficult reintegration after the dark years of persecution. The progression from witch's familiar to the lord of the house, which is the status it occupies now (pointless to pretend otherwise), has been slow and governed by many complex factors, the main one being health. The cat again came to our attention as we realized the connection between diseases and their carriers, especially rodents. The age-old antagonism between cat and mouse, which was probably first made use of in ancient Egypt, became of fundamental importance again, this time not only to protect the granaries but, more importantly, to protect man from disease. Proof

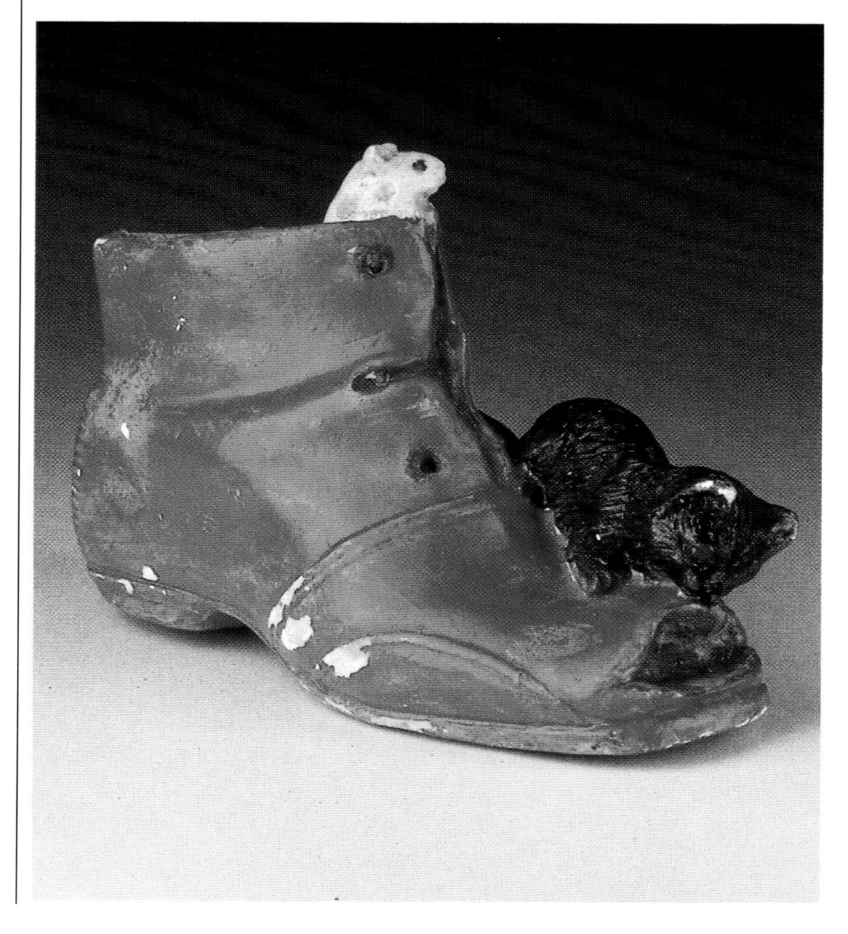

The modern cat above is in cloisonné enamel, a technique used by the Chinese for centuries on plates and vases. The nineteenth-century boot opposite with a kitten and a mouse is in biscuit.

of their ability was given by the hunting cats in the English colonies of America when they repelled the rodents' onslaught on the colonies' harvest. But the evidence that convinced even the most cynical was furnished by the cats in Egypt itself when the first signs of the plague spread throughout the corps of the Napoleonic expedition. All it took to stop the spread was a squadron of cats to bring the mice in the army encampment under control and thereby limit the breeding ground of infection. The most extraordinary thing is that all this happened under the

command of Napoleon who was one of the most famous cat haters of all. It is a well-known fact that the only time he called "Guards!" with a tone of panic in his voice was not to save himself from assassination, but because a cat had got into the imperial apartments. To be fair, the great Corsican may well have suffered from a phobia of or allergy to cats so that the merest approach of a cat would have caused him much distress.

Further progress towards the reinstatement of cats was aided by the newly dominant middle class. The aristocracy favoured country houses and large mansions in the cities, often with gardens. They could therefore have many animals as companions: dogs, horses, falcons, small decorative birds, etc. The middle classes, instead, lived in town houses, often divided into apartments, near the shops

Below, a plush kitten from the 1950s. The Peter Fagan Collection contains a series of small hand-painted, resin models, the Home Sweet Home series. One of the prettiest pieces is the fireplace with two little cats opposite.

or their businesses. This was not a way of life adapted to the needs of domestic animals requiring constant access to space in which to wander. On the other hand, which companionable animal can adapt itself to the space available, will come and go even across roofs, grooms itself, often more fastidiously than its owners, and leaves no tracks or nasty smells? The cat, of course. It seemed to have been created precisely for the type of life style that the town-dwelling man of the industrial revolution had adopted. As a gentle companion to children and adults alike it had few competitors: the only ones worth mentioning were small dogs, or more specifically lapdogs.

And so it was that our friend, with its habitual dignity and phlegm, took back the coveted post. It jumped on the armchair and crouched by the fireside as if it had been doing nothing else all its life, without whining, without howling, responding with signs of aloof contentment to the hand that caressed it, provided that it wished to be caressed, of course.

Next came a deep interest in the breeding and raising of these pets (though actually quite late in the period of feline-human cohabitation). The work of identification of breeds and selection and the inevitable competitions soon followed.

The interest of intellectuals, writers, poets, artists, was naturally aroused, all attracted by the god-like movements, the independence of character and the dignity of His Excellency the mouser. The cat's prolific breeding capacity and the limited number of homes provided by townspeople produced almost immediately another phenomenon: that of the return of the cat to a semi-wild state within the city walls.

This Italian carving from the 1950s is in teak. The jar opposite is in rose biscuit from France. The delightful teapot and milk jug on the preceding pages are modern Chinese.

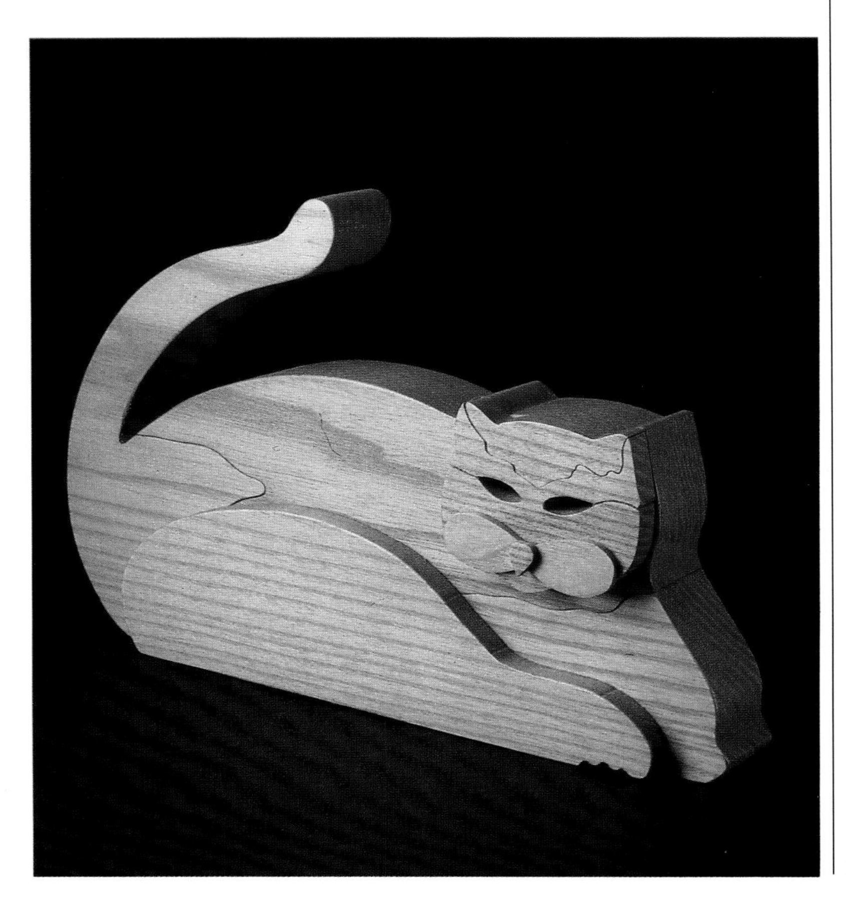

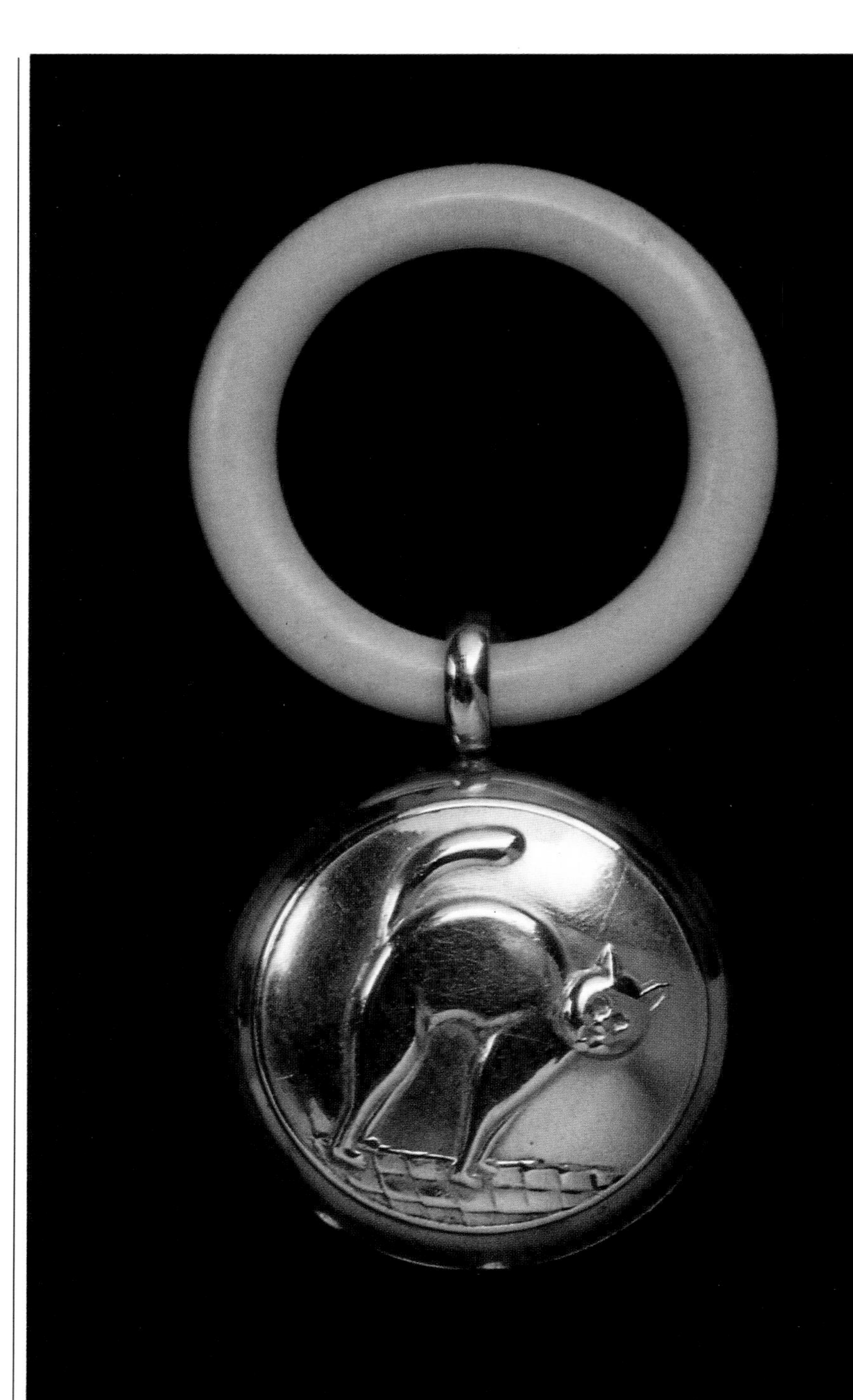

The stray has nothing to do with the wild cat: it is smaller (usually leaner and thinner than a house-based cat) and has no difficulty in returning to the domestic state, if only someone offers it the chance. But what is new about this cat is that, after centuries of solitary life in the wild and a long life as a domestic loner, the city stray – by the sheer will to survive – has learnt to live in communities, on waste ground or in the basements of derelict houses. And the social stray has, in its turn, given rise to a new type of person in our communities: the blessed person, often single, who looks after a whole tribe of cats, bringing them their food to the same place and at the same time, every day. Recent ethological studies have examined life and social relationships within a group of stray cats. No one has systematically investigated the life of those who feed them. We all know from experience that they are, for the most part, older people, perhaps finding relief from their own loneliness. There is probably no need to know any more. They are guardian angels and that is enough.

The cat as a child's companion, again: this rattle in silver with an ivory ring is a beautiful example of goldsmiths' ailurophilia.

In spite of its oriental look this china kitten is Italian. The theme of the playful kitten has a universal appeal as many shopkeepers know. They often put models like this in their windows to attract passersby.

Friends and enemies

All this takes us back to the original theme – the cat as a domestic animal. Or, to be more precise, to cat and human living together. In this arrangement one thing is very clear: it is a partnership on unequal terms in which qualities of dignity, independence and self-control are all on one side. Of the human and the cat, which of the two meticulously grooms himself every day, who is impeccably clean to the point of concealing his own excrement and who never shows off? Which of the two, on the contrary, shows the greater signs of needing the other, calling to it, talking continuously and often incoherently to it? There can be no doubt. It is the human, or the subspecies the cat lover, who needs the cat, not the other way around. Naturally, the cat lover will deny all the evidence and ridiculously exaggerate the animal's scant demonstrations of affection, silently passing over the unending displays of egotism on the cat's part. When it comes down to it, the human raises not the least objection if the kitty decides to sleep on his bed, and he has to spend all night in an uncomfortable position to accommodate it.

When you try to seat a guest in the cat's favourite armchair it will start to circle around with an air of outrage, to mew, to jump from the back of the chair to the arms, to give every possible sign of displeasure. It will use every form of persuasion to get its armchair back, refusing to go to sleep somewhere else. Tame cats put out claws only if constrained to do so but otherwise every means short of violence will be considered for motives of defense against attack by third parties or against over-insistent demonstrations of affection.

If you succeed in bringing the cat lover back to a semblance of objective rationality, she will still admit that she has no answer to the question that bothers anyone who has had to do with cats. When cats give the clearest sign of approval of which they are capable, making a noise like the engine of a car left in neutral, and when that purring becomes more intense, verging on the ecstatic, is it a sign of

The eternal conjecture: is the cat more fond of its home than of its owner? It certainly loves an armchair and will vie for the seat rather than the back, as this hand-painted model from the Peter Fagan Collection shows.

affection and gratitude towards the person who has just served up its favourite dish, or keeps it warm by sitting with it on the sofa, or saves it the trouble of scratching itself by passing a finger lightly over its head just in the right place? Or is it not rather an uncontrollable sign of self-satisfaction, as if to say: "Well, old chap, we've done it again, we've got ourselves a good meal and a place in the warm and, if we put up with this interfering biped always rearranging our coat, we've got a good chance of having the same treatment in the days and years to come."?

And while there is no way of knowing the answer to this, there has certainly never been a shortage of cat lovers. Highly gifted people seem to have a particular propensity for falling into such relationships of mutual dependence. Think of writers who have had one or more cats: Dr Samuel Johnson, who went out himself to buy oysters for Hodge, in case the servants resented having to run errands for a cat and would be unkind to it behind the doctor's back; Dickens, Baudelaire, Emil Zola, Henry James and Ernest Hemingway were all crazy about cats. The French writer Colette, author of *The Cat*, lived with dozens of these pets. An interviewer once counted two score of them. But it was, above all, Aldous Huxley who put the case for this rapport when a young aspiring writer asked him the secret of becoming a successful author. "So you would like to write," said Huxley thoughtfully, looking his young interlocutor up and down. "Well, start by getting a cat."

There are good relationships between our heroes and scientists. A case of early ailurophilia is that of Sir Isaac Newton, the discoverer of gravity, who made a cat-flap in the door of his house for his own cats to come and go without distracting him from his work. It seems he had two cats, one large and one small, and so he made two openings

in the door. It escaped one of the fathers of modern science that, while the large cat could not get through the small hole, the little cat would have no difficulty in going through the large one. Sharing these feelings are such famous personalities as Pasteur, Einstein and Albert Schweitzer. Indeed, the respect that all cats have (except in moments of acute hunger) for the silence of the scientist and the poet is a quality that all kinds of scholars greatly appreciate. A case in point is *St Jerome in his Study* painted around 1474 by Antonello da Massina, which shows, only a few feet away from the writing saint, a beautiful tabby cat asleep. Nor is the saint disturbed by the peacock and the partridge in the foreground, perhaps because they are other quiet creatures. Even a big cat in the form of a lion, which roams about in the shadows of the room while he is working, does not disturb him.

Much could be written about the affinity between the cat and wisdom. But there is another closer, more intimate relationship between the cat and popular wisdom, expressed most clearly in the wide range of proverbs. Almost all languages have a substantial collection of almost universal sayings with a feline context: all cats are grey in the dark, is typical. An impressive compendium of wisdom (and iconography, as the text in various editions is illustrated) is presented in the collection of the Dutch poet and statesman,

Although Art Deco in style, this Italian container of Mau wax was made in 1946. By contrast, the little picture opposite, signed by Cipriano, is naive. The cats on the preceding pages are from all over the world.

Jacob Cats (would you believe it?), first published in 1632, with pictures by the greatest painter and engraver of the time, Adriaen Pietersz van de Venne. The work is called *Spiegel van den ouden ende nieuwen tydt*, and the book's importance has been stressed by the great student of feline art and history, Elizabeth Foucart-Walter, curator of the Department of Painting at the Louvre.

Jacob Cats collected moralistic proverbs from many languages and van de Venne illustrated them often using cats. Some pictures use cats as the actual subject and others have slightly more esoteric depictions, while all tell a moral tale. One shows a cat licking a candle close to a young man who is assiduously paying court to a lady, not young nor beautiful, but widowed and heiress to a large fortune. The

Have you ever heard of a guard-cat? The cat decorating this china candlestick from the 1920s seems to be keeping guard over its candle. And yet, according to Jacob Cats, they hated them.

moral is: opportunistic fortune hunters are like cats – they lick candles even though they hate them. More overt is a small picture showing a lady using tongs to beat a cat that has moved too close to the cooking pot: "A greedy cat gets a blow on the nose," says the French proverb, warning us not to be too inquisitive.

"Let the fine cat beware of the furrier," and in this case it is the engraving that clarifies the meaning of the words. Here we see a louche figure with a sack approaching a sleeping cat, but in the background another scene is being played out, this time one of seduction. A young and beautiful girl is courted by an elegant gentleman. The comparison of the two scenes invites young girls of marrying age to take care: they could be of interest only for their beauty.

In Jacob Cats's collection there is a moral for everything. A man marches proudly with a bunch of cats, carrying on his shoulder a pike laden with big rats. The proverb explains that "He who hunts with cats only catches rats," or as we say "Let the cobbler stick to his last." Finally, a medallion shows a cat leaping here and there, all over a room literally laid waste by a man who is after it with a sword. Jacob Cats tells us that this state of affairs is due to a wife asking her husband to do away with a cat that had become intolerable. And, looking at the state of the house, the message emerges that some enterprises are better abandoned before damage becomes irreparable.

The history of popular engravings is perhaps richer in cat subjects than painting itself, though the latter has plenty of felines by its artists, from Ghirlandaio to Rembrandt, Renoir, Matisse, and great contemporaries like David Hockney. La Fontaine's *Fables* are profusely illustrated, while there is no shortage either of polemical works based

These kittens, experts at creating havoc, are on a card dated 1903, the golden age for "cat" cards. Quiet and pensive is the cat opposite by a contemporary Chinese artist, who has used the refined and old technique of painting porcelain with enamel.

on the theme of the cat–mouse war. Possibly the most representative example comes from the city of Arras whose inhabitants were nicknamed "rats," either in association with the name of their native town, or because of the mice on the coat-of-arms on the bishop's palace. During the Thirty Years War Arras was in a long drawn-out contest between the Spaniards and the French; "When the rats eat the cats the French will enter Arras," was a piece of Spanish propaganda during the time the town was in Iberian hands. But when Richelieu entered Arras at the head of the French army in August 1640, there soon appeared an engraving showing a regal cat adorned with a frilled ruff, with the caption: "The French have taken Arras, and the rats have not eaten the cats." In successive stages the rats went over to the French side, and the cats became Spanish. So, for once, an engraving of 1641 shows a feline army vanquished by rodent infantry.

The relationship between cats and painters, no less than that with writers, has an easy explanation; rats appreciate a canvas, painted or not (even unused canvases cost money!), just as much as a plate of food.

In Austria at the height of its power decorative cats were very popular. In this bronze nineteenth-century work two minstrel cats swing together on the moon.

The connection between our four-pawed friends and the greats of history has had more ups and downs. We have already shown two significant examples: the ailurophile (Richelieu) and the ailurophobe (Napoleon). Those who have lived happily with cats include Frederick the Great, Queen Victoria and Pope Leo XII. The last had a cat called Micetto which outlived him and was adopted by the French ambassador, a chap called Châteaubriand! Among cat haters, or at least those who were indifferent to them, were Julius Caesar, Genghis Khan and Mussolini. They might have changed their views had they been aware of a modern medical theory, supported by appropriate statistical data, according to which the cohabitation of man and cat is good for both, in the sense that the domestic cat lives infinitely longer than the stray or feral cat (which, poor creature, has a somewhat reduced life expectancy), while men or women with a cat or cats have, for their part, a better life expectancy than those who have none.

There is an explanation for this second aspect. The cat is an animal particularly adapted to living with elderly, even infirm, people. It provides company, keeps its human cotenants busy, and constrains them to a certain regularity in their lives. Moreover, it lets itself be looked after with a minimum of physical effort. For anyone with heart trouble, a cat is a thousand times better than having an energetic and excitable dog with the inescapable obligation to take it for walks (or hikes) every day.

In statistical terms: around 33 per cent of cat lovers are expected to live longer than average; in the case of dog lovers, possibly due to the daily excursions, the figure drops straight down to 10 per cent.

Furthermore, there are characteristics of a cat's nature that induce a meditative, tranquil life, which beyond a certain age is certainly healthier.

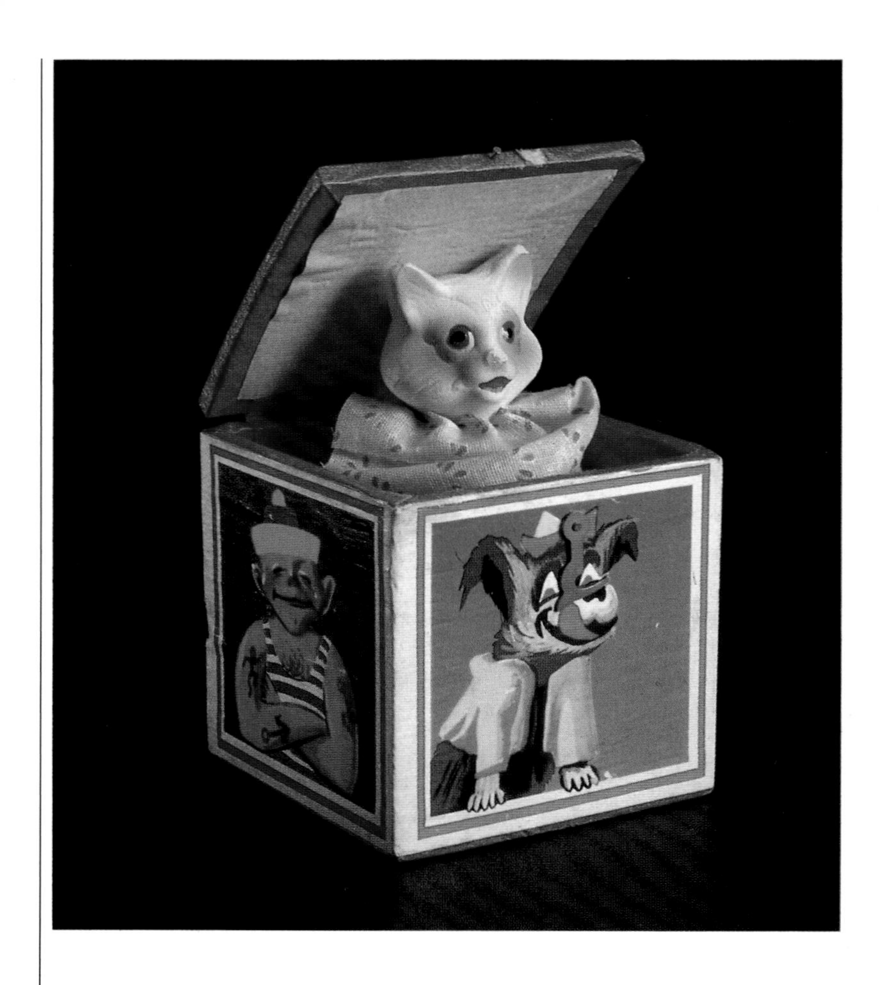

Universally popular, playing kittens. This fine jack-in-the-box must have provided amusement for many children and adults alike.

Still on the subject of a quiet and regular life, it is, of course, a well-known fact that in a domestic cat's ideal environment above all nothing must change. Secondly, there should be reasonable silence around the house, or at least peace from really disturbing noises. The first condition excludes any impulsive rearrangements of the decor:

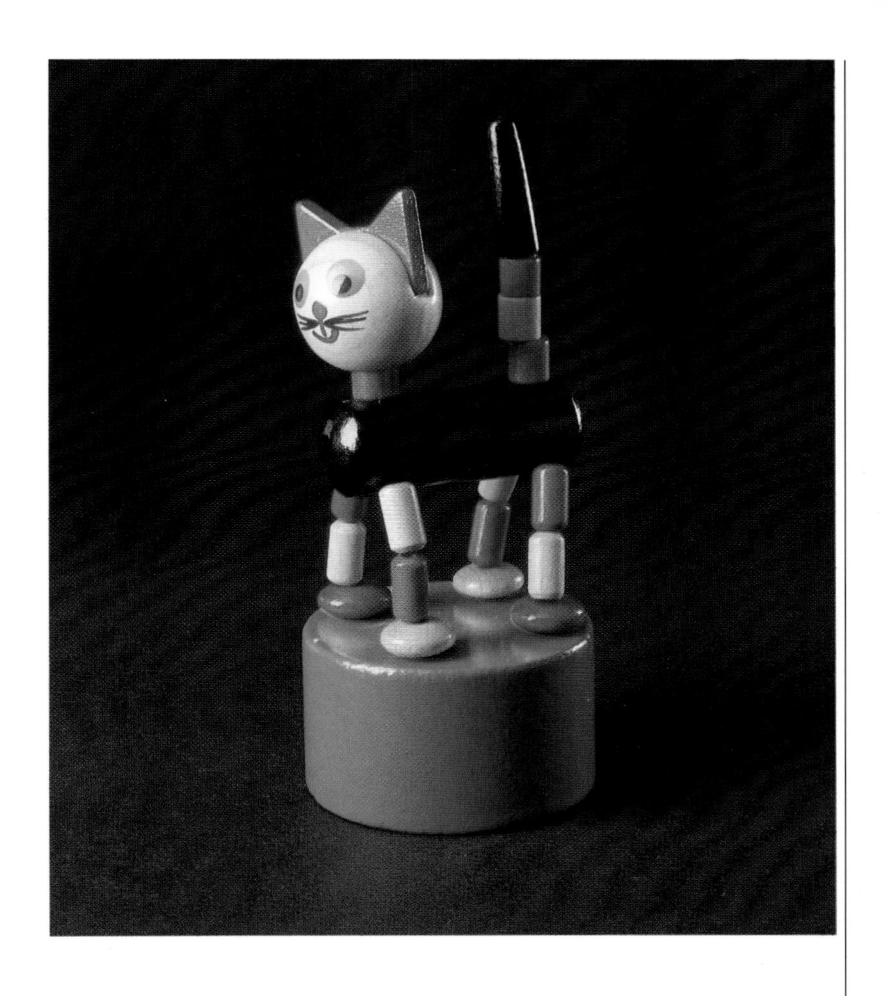

This disjointed cat is probably for older children. It is a classic from the 1950s. The head, tail and joints collapse when the base is pressed.

moving the furniture around every six months or buying new pieces too frequently will obviously provoke great disapproval from your cat. The same haughty objection may be caused by over-frequent changes in members of the household. For example, if cat lovers do not wish to incur the disfavour of their companion, they should avoid a busy love life, either that or practise it away from home.

Yet this creature of silence and tranquillity is ready to make compromises when a baby arrives in the house. A few millennia of experience as a baby-sitter have left their mark and it is common to see a cat put up with behaviour from the newborn that, if inflicted by an adult, would immediately make it want to return to the wild. Such tolerance, however, is not automatically extended to baby's peer group. When the little ones get together in a group for an outing or a birthday party, the cat may be seen escaping into some of the most extraordinary hiding places imaginable: slipping along the wall making itself

indistinguishable from the wallpaper; lying under an armchair a few inches high; sliding out of the house through gaps that most snakes would have difficulty negotiating.

It is on such occasions that the wisdom of the cat is most apparent. Given that the mixing of small, wild bipeds and a member of the feline race must willy-nilly end in tears, in total disarray with reproaches and exchanges of blows, it is obviously much more prudent to abandon the game before it even starts. In the mouser's genetic memory there seems to be an imprint, according to which the gathering together of man's little ones leads to noise, damage and the moving of furniture – all mishaps that it detests to the depths of its soul. Rather than stay around, for once grimalkin prefers to relinquish its proverbial (and usually unassailable) dignity and march off disguised by the wall.

A cat's life is not exclusively divided between idle domesticity and the more adventurous and dangerous existence of a wild cat. The old tradition that the cat should earn its keep by defending the foodstuff from raids by rodents often still holds good. One of the most remarkable cases, which occurred in 1961, is that of the hundreds of cats caught in Singapore and dropped by parachute over Borneo to save the harvest.

Concerned enough by rats to have cats entered on the list of regular staff, are the postal authorities of various countries, including Great Britain, the United States and Denmark. New Zealand also, until quite recently, had cats on the government pay-roll. Some mousers have contributed to the conquest of space: it was the French who carefully trained a little cat and then sent it off several tens of thousands of miles into space, on board the spaceship *Véronique*. The cat in question was trained, among other things – no one knows how – to remain absolutely still for long periods of time. Cat lovers and animal lovers in general

It is difficult, if not impossible, to make a cat work. It is very easy, on the other hand, to find it curled up inside a basket, as in this pretty French ceramic.

The contemporary Italian potter, Verzolini, made this perplexed-looking cat. Somewhat older, from the 1930s, is this china lemon-squeezer cat.

literally become enraged even to hear mention of it and it sounds cruel enough to upset even the hard-hearted, but let us not forget that there are also cats submitted to laboratory experiments for the sake of medical research. Cats do not represent good subjects for research in all fields, but it seems that as far as the study of the circulation of the blood is concerned, and also nervous diseases, it has to be feline victims that are sacrificed on the altar of our health. If this argument seems disagreeable, history records an even more idiotic use devised by humans for cats.

In 1968 the American forces decided that because cats can see well in dim light, the proverbial virtue of felines, they could have first-rate tactical uses. Several cats were trained in the United States and then sent to Vietnam. The officials who made these decisions could never have had cats of their own living with them, otherwise they could easily have foreseen that it would end in total disaster.

In America there is a study on everything and therefore it should be no surprise that two researchers, Aline and Robert Kidd, have interviewed dozens of people who live with dogs, cats and other animals, to get their identikit picture or psychological profile. The work enables us to present a pretty good sketch of the cat lover.

Those who live with cats greatly resemble their animals. Compared with dog owners they are more fond of the quiet life; they especially dislike crowds, large parties and popular, noisy events. They are more impervious than most to fashions, and more inclined to live their own lives as they see fit. The greatest difference by comparison with dog lovers lies in their approach to life's problems, and particularly those relating to work. Dog owners face things head-on, from the front and, where there are differences of opinion, do all they can to impose their own point of view. Such a confrontational attitude horrifies those who live with cats. It is not that they recoil from difficulties, just that they do everything possible to steer clear of them, seeking to follow their own path in spite of impediments. When they do meet an apparently insuperable obstacle, cat people (those who have learned how to live from a cat) withdraw in great style, leaving the field free. When things turn sour, they simply change where they work, how they live or what they do, as if to say "If that's the way they want it, let them have it. If there is nothing to be done, why bother to argue." An eminently feline philosophy: in many cases mousers must be proud of their owners. The cat lover is not enthusiastic about small children (only 30 per cent say they like them) and is not particularly overjoyed by the company of a group of adolescents (15 per cent do not like them). Self-reliance and independence rank high in the cat owner's scale of values; there is little inclination to become involved in the lives of others. Similarly, men with aggressive voices score low, as do women with shrill ones. In other words, those who have absorbed the rules of cat living wish neither

Below, two nineteenth-century bronze figures from Austria. The wooden toy opposite could be Felix. Made in England, it dates from the 1920s. The Art Deco vase on the following pages, made in the 1930s, is from Czechoslovakia.

to dominate nor to be dominated. They prefer freedom to dependence and tranquillity to having their own way.

Believing in statistics leads to well-founded mistakes as marketing experts, who spend their lives doing nothing else, know. And even this profile of the cat's human friend seems too neat – too cat-like – to be true. It may well be that the answers given to the researchers correspond not to what the cat lovers really are, but rather to what they would like to be. Once more man's relationship with the cat is transferred from the world of reality to that of projections and it is the cat that is revealed as the protagonist in this alliance. People keep a cat as a pet, a companion and a cohabitant but the terms of the partnership are determined by the cat's personality, not theirs.

The amazing fact is that it has maintained this personality, almost unchanged, across the centuries and through changes of status. Again we are compelled to borrow from magic, simply because it is impossible to find a rational explanation for such behaviour in the theories available. Our feline

friend, from when it decided to join human society, has adapted itself to the most varied circumstances, even performing a last most difficult transformation to find a place beside mankind in industrial civilization. This long journey has been completed with a minimum of changes. *Felis cattus* seems to have travelled through history, allowing itself to be lightly touched by it, being little influenced, and deigning to take very little interest. If we try to seek answers from its mysterious eyes, we obtain the age-old sibylline response. In that retina appears our own image, surrounded by those flashes of light that so impressed witches and inquisitors. Herein, perhaps, lies the secret of the cat: knowing how to be, in terms of sensuousness, agility, dignity and infinite grace, what we ourselves would like to be, if only we could live, not in the real world, but in the one we see reflected in those luminous eyes.

The silver mask brooch above is truly striking. One of the most famous cats of all is Puss in Boots, from the fairy tale of the same name. It inspired the little figure opposite from the 1940s.

Literary cats

Literature is full of cats: partly, perhaps, because they stimulate the writer's imagination, but mostly, because there are few writers who have not had a cat. Lope de Vega dedicated to the feline world his epic poem, *La Gattomaquia*, in which he gives his cats such melodious names as Mizifuf, Marramaquiz and Zappaquilda. However, it is in modern times that the link between the cat and literature has been more strongly forged. One can picture Homer without a cat, but definitely not Ernest Hemingway. From the first century up to today, few poets escaped feline fascination. There is no lack of examples of cat protagonists. Rudyard Kipling's famous story, *The Cat that Walked by Itself*, is a hypothetical, but possible, account of a relationship beginning between man and cat. It is the tale of a cat that turns up in a cave inhabited by humans and offers to join the community, laying down, however, a considerable number of conditions, among them the right to go out alone during the night to wander where it will. The emergence of a fast increasing number of cat lovers can be deduced from the large number of literary works with "cat" in the title, even if it has nothing to do with the text: *Cat on a Hot Tin Roof* by Tennessee Williams is one of many examples. But we are interested in the writers and poets who have written specifically about cats so here, then, is a little anthology.

Is it books that like cats, or cats that like books? Let us leave the question to cats and readers. They are certainly on good terms, as this delightful English pussy cat by Peter Fagan shows.

MEDIEVAL PROVERB

Catus amat pisces, sed non vult tingere plantas. [The cat would eat fish, but would not wet her feet.]

JACOBUS DIACONUS, **The Life of St Gregory the Great**

Gregory I the Great (*b.* c. 540; *d.* 604), once Prefect of Rome, was the greatest of the sixteen popes of that name. He was a master of prose and through his writings – which are still published – wielded great influence on the Middle Ages, before he left public life;

– He possessed nothing in the world except a cat, which he carried in his bosom, frequently caressing it, as his sole companion.

GEOFFREY CHAUCER, **The Maunciple's Tale**

Swiche Appetit Hath She
Let take a cat, and foster hire with milke
And tendre flesh, and make hire couche of
silke,
And let hire see a mous go by the wall,
Anon she weiveth milke and flesh, and all,
And every deintee that is in the hous,
Swiche appetit hath she to ete the mous.

MICHEL DE MONTAIGNE

When I play with my cat, who knows whether I do not make her more sport than she makes me?

Here is another model from the Home Sweet Home series. Poets have not limited themselves to writing about cats, but have shown great dedication to them too, as Jean Cocteau's design opposite for the Club des Amis des Chats demonstrates.

Picture postcards were extremely popular at the beginning of the twentieth century and cats were a favourite subject. Here we see a little feline hunter (but what will happen to the chicks?) on a French card dated 1904.

JAMES BOSWELL, **Life of Dr Johnson**

I will never forget the indulgence with which Dr Johnson treated his cat, Hodge, for whom he himself use to go out and buy oysters lest the servants, having that trouble, should take a dislike to the poor creature. I am unluckily one of those who have an antipathy to cats, so that I am uneasy when in the room with one, and I own I frequently suffered a good deal from the presence of the same Hodge. I remember him one day scrambling up Dr Johnson's breast apparently with much satisfaction while my friend, smiling and half-whistling, rubbed down his back and pulled him by the tail and when I observed he was a fine cat, saying, "Why yes, sir, but I have had cats that I liked better than this," and then, as if perceiving Hodge to be out of countenance, adding, "but he is a very fine cat, a very fine cat indeed."

James Boswell, writing this Life of Dr Johnson*, must have suffered exceedingly in the process, having to put up with Hodge, but he got his own back in his poem on matrimony.*

A Matrimonial Thought

In the blithe days of honeymoon,
With Kate's allurements smitten,
I lov'd her late, I lov'd her soon,
And call'd her dearest kitten.

But now my kitten's grown a cat,
And cross like other wives,
O! by my soul, my honest Mat,
I fear she has nine lives.

A. C. SWINBURNE, **To a Cat**

Other writers, on the other hand, have written more lovingly about cats.

Stately, kindly, lordly friend,
– Condescend
Here to sit by me and turn

Glorious eyes that smile and burn,
Golden eyes, love's lustruous meed,
On the golden page I read.

The link between catmania and literature can be seen in the nineteenth-century ink-well below, used, perhaps, by a writer who took his inspiration from cats. Opposite, Krazy Kat hit by a brick; a recurring episode in the strip cartoon by George Herriman.

JOHN KEATS, **To Mrs Reynold's Cat**

Gaze / With those bright languid segments green, and prick
Those velvet ears – but pr'ythee do not stick
Thy latent talons in me – and upraise
Thy gentle mew – and tell me all thy frays,
Of fish and mice, and rats and tender chick.

A. S. J. TESSIMOND, extract from **Cats**

In this verse A. S. J. Tessimond captures the essence of felinity.

Cats, no less liquid than their shadows,
Offer no angles to the wind,
They slip, diminished, neat, through loopholes
Less than themselves; will not be pinned
To rules or routes for journeys; . . .

MICHAEL JOSEPH, **To a Siamese Cat**

In this poem the publisher Michael Joseph wrote one of the most moving to Charles.

I shall walk in the sun alone
Whose golden light you loved:
I shall sleep alone
And, stirring, touch an empty place:
I shall write uninterrupted
(Would that your gentle paw
Could stay my moving pen just once
  again!)
I shall see beauty
But none to match your living grace:
I shall hear music
But not so sweet as the droning song
With which you loved me.
I shall fill my days
But I shall not, cannot forget:
Sleep soft, dear friend,
For while I live you shall not die.

GUILLAUME APOLLINAIRE, **The Cat** from **Bestiary**

*Guillaume Apollinaire, born Wilhelm Apollinaris de Kostrowitzki (*b. *Rome 1880;* d. *Paris 1918), was one of the leaders of the new movement in poetry that was sweeping through the whole of Europe. He freed poetry from its traditional disciplines, including that of punctuation. His own work is direct, sincere and sensitive.*

Je souhaite dans ma maison:
Une femme ayant sa raison,
Un chat passant parmi les livres,
Des amis en tout saison
Sans lesquels je ne peux pas vivre.

[In my house I want a reasonable woman,/A cat passing among the books,/ And friends in every season/Without whom I cannot live.]

Following in the footsteps of Don Quixote, the kittens on this card tilt at a windmill, even if it is really only a clock. The card is French from 1907.

EDGAR ALLAN POE, **The Black Cat** from **Tales**

One of the great masters of the horror story, Edgar Allan Poe (1809–1849) has written a terrifying short story about a black cat. Its owner, a man ruined by vice, comes to hate it and tries to kill it with an axe but, instead, kills his wife who is trying to stop him. He walls up her corpse in the cellar not noticing that the cat has slipped behind the bricks. When the police become suspicious, they visit the house and it is the cat's howls that lead them to the discovery of the dead body.

One night as I sat half stupefied in a den of more than infamy, my attention was suddenly drawn to some black object reposing upon the head of one of the immense hogsheads of gin or rum which constituted the chief furniture of the apartment. I had been looking steadily at the top of this hogshead for some minutes, and what now caused me surprise was the fact that I had not sooner perceived the object thereupon. I approached it, and touched it with my hand. It was a black cat, a very large one, fully as large as Pluto, and closely resembling him in every respect but one. Pluto had not a white hair upon any portion of his body; but this cat had a large, although indefinite, splotch of white, covering nearly the whole region of the breast.

Upon my touching him, he immediately arose, purred loudly, rubbed against my hand, and appeared delighted with my notice. This, then, was the very creature of which I was in search. I at once offered to purchase it of the landlord; but this person made no claim to it – knew nothing of it – had never seen it before.

I continued my caresses; and when I prepared to go home, the animal evinced a disposition to accompany me. I permitted

it to do so, occasionally stooping and patting it as I proceeded. When it reached the house it domesticated itself at once, and became immediately a great favourite with my wife.

For my own part, I soon found a dislike to it arising within me. This was just the reverse of what I had anticipated; but – I know not how or why it was – its evident fondness for myself rather disgusted and annoyed. By slow degrees these feelings of disgust and annoyance rose into the bitterness of hatred. I avoided the creature; a certain sense of shame, and the remembrance of my former deed of cruelty, prevented me from physically abusing it. I did not for some weeks strike it or otherwise violently ill-use it; but gradually – very gradually – I came to look upon it with unutterable loathing, and to flee silently from its odious presence, as from the breath of a pestilence.

T. S. ELIOT, **The Naming of Cats**

T. S. Eliot was born in 1888 in St Louis, Missouri, and died in London in 1965. One of the most influential poets and critics of the century, possibly his most endearing work is Old Possum's Book of Practical Cats *(published 1939), a collection of nonsense rhymes for children that was equally popular with adults. Andrew Lloyd Webber, with a team of exceptionally acrobatic dancers, singers and actors, turned it into the highly successful musical* Cats. *Below is the first poem from* Old Possum's Book.

The Naming of Cats is a difficult matter,
  It isn't just one of your holiday games;
You may think at first I'm as mad as a hatter
  When I tell you, a cat must have THREE DIFFERENT NAMES.
First of all, there's the name that the family use daily,
  Such as Peter, Augustus, Alonzo or James,
Such as Victor or Jonathan, George or Bill Bailey –
  All of them sensible everyday names.
There are fancier names if you think they sound sweeter,
  Some for the gentlemen, some for the dames:
Such as Plato, Admetus, Electra, Demeter –
  But all of them sensible everyday names.

Below, Felix, famous cartoon cat, in full swing. A splendid example of a literary and fantastic mouser is the Cheshire Cat from Lewis Carroll's Alice in Wonderland. *The drawing opposite by John Tenniel is from the first edition of 1865.*

But I tell you, a cat needs a name that's particular,
A name that's peculiar, and more dignified,
Else how can he keep up his tail perpendicular,
Or spread out his whiskers, or cherish his pride?
Of names of this kind, I can give you a quorum,
Such as Munkustrap, Quaxo, or Coricopat,
Such as Bombalurina, or else Jellylorum –
Names that never belong to more than one cat.
But above and beyond there's still one name left over,
And that is the name that you never will guess;
The name that no human research can discover –
But THE CAT HIMSELF KNOWS, and will never confess.
When you notice a cat in profound meditation,
The reason, I tell you, is always the same:
His mind is engaged in a rapt contemplation
Of the thought, of the thought, of the thought of his name:
His ineffable effable
Effanineffable
Deep and inscrutable singular Name.

This life-sized English door stopper in enamelled cast iron astonishes and petrifies all dogs that come across it.

T. H. HUXLEY, **Letter**

Thomas Henry Huxley (1825–1895), the biologist, was a great man of science who liked to have cats around him. In a letter to a friend he described his cat.

A long series of cats has reigned over my household for the last forty years or thereabouts. The present occupant of the throne is a large, young, grey Tabby – Oliver by name. Not that he is in any sense a Protector, for I doubt whether he has the heart to kill a mouse. However, I saw him catch and eat the first butterfly of the season, and trust that the germ of courage, thus manifested, may develop with age into efficient mousing.

As to sagacity, I should say that his judgment respecting the warmest place and the softest cushion in a room is infallible, his punctuality at meal times is admirable, and his pertinacity in jumping on people's shoulders till they give him some of the best of what is going, indicates great firmness.

Household words the world over

Brief glossary of cats in four languages

English

cat *n.* [from Old English *catte*] a carnivore of genus *Felis* || *(informal)* a spiteful woman; a showily-dressed man; a jazz fan || (*adj.*) *cat-like*, stealthy, noiseless || *cat's paw*, one who is manipulated by another || *cat-suit*, a one-piece trouser suit || *cat-walk*, a narrow footway || *bell the cat*, to take the leading part in a hazardous venture, from the fable of the mice who wished to hang a warning bell around the cat's neck || *cat nap*, a short sleep || *cat's meat*, horse's flesh sold for cats || *cat-o'-nine-tails*, a whip with nine knotted ends, once used in the navy and the army || *to let the cat out of the bag*, to reveal a secret || *to be like cat and dog*, to quarrel continuously || *enough to make a cat laugh*, to make even the least inclined laugh || *like something the cat brought in*, bedraggled || *the cat's pyjamas, the cat's whiskers*, anything very good, just what is wanted || *no room to swing a cat*, a minimum of space || *to rain cats and dogs*, to rain very heavily.

French

chat *n.m.* [from the Latin *cattus*] cat || *mon petit chat*, my dear, my pet || *acheter chat en poche*, to buy a pig in a poke || *appeler un chat un chat*, to call a spade a spade || *arriver dès les chats*, to come home with the milk, in the small hours || *avoir un chat dans la gorge*, to have a frog in one's throat || *écrire comme un chat*, to write illegibly, to scrawl || *être comme chat sur braise*, to be like a cat on hot bricks || *donner sa langue aux chats*, to give up guessing || *à bon chat, bon rat*, tit for tat || *chat échaudé craint l'eau*, once bitten, twice shy || *chat à neuf queues*, cat-o'-nine-tails || *il n'y a si petit chat qui n'égratigne*, even a worm will turn.

German

Katze *n.f.* cat || (*informal*) puss || *falsch wie eine Katze*, false as a serpent, treacherous || *bei Nacht sind alle Katzen grau*, all cats are grey in the dark || *die Katze im Sack kaufen*, to buy a pig in a poke || *die Katze aus dem Sack lassen*, to let the

It is not always true that learning favours dialogue. Here, for example, the books are divided by the never-ending quarrels between dog and cat. These wooden book ends date from the early twentieth century.

cat out of the bag, to reveal a secret || *wie die Katze um den heißen Brei gehen*, to beat about the bush || *das ist für die Katze*, that is useless, a complete waste || *neunschwanzige Katze*, cat-o'-nine-tails.

Italian

gatto *n.m.*[from the Latin *Felis cattus*] cat || *(informal) prendersi una gatta da pelare*, to face a difficult task without reward or without obligation || *avere il gatto nella madia*, to have the wolf at the door || *gatta ci cova*, there's something brewing, something in the wind || *gattabuia*, prison, jail || *gattamorta*, a sly, wily person || *essere come cane e gatto*, quarrelling savagely || *eravamo in quattro gatti*, there was hardly anyone there || *gatto di piomba*, a clumsy person || *gatto scottato dall'acqua calda, ha paura della fredda*, once bitten, twice shy || *avere gli occhi da gatto*, to be cat-eyed, keen sighted || *occhio di gatto*, cat's eye, any of a group of gemstones, a yellowish-green type of chrysoberyl that reflects a streak of light when cut in a rounded shape || *gatto a nove code*, cat-o'-nine-tails.

Acknowledgements
This book would not have been possible without the contributions of many cat lovers. The author wishes to thank the owners of objects photographed, and the following:
Valeria Alessandri Di Guida (Il Gatto, Milan)
Maurizio Epifani (L'oso dei farlocchi, Milan)
Rosella Pisciotta, Luigi Sapino (Galleria Mirabilia, Turin)
Eugenio Zucco (La Giostra, Turin)

The publisher thanks Gruppo Mantero for allowing the reproduction of the Interseta design on the jacket.

Page 6: china cat by Merit of Germany.
Pages 40 and 41: porcelain cat by Goebel of Germany
Page 73: Mau wax tin from Wagner of Monfalcone

Picture sources
The cats illustrated in this book belong to the following collections:
Zanze Baroni Borgese (pp. 19, 30–31, 35, 43, 54–55, 56, 62, 79, 82, 85, 91, 109);
Susanna Gang Crivelli (jacket, pp. 10–11, 12, 20, 28, 34, 37, 44, 45, 51, 53, 70–71, 72, 77);
Eliana Pollana (pp. 2, 7, 8, 9, 13, 14, 15, 16–17, 18, 21, 22, 25, 26, 27, 29, 33, 75, 76, 80, 81, 84, 86, 89, 90, 92–93, 94, 95, 96, 99, 100, 102, 105, 111);
Gabriella Trager (pp. 56, 67).

All photographs by Giorgio Coppin in collaboration with Anna Giorgetti.